YŪSUF *and the* LOTUS FLOWER

Poems

Doyali Farah Islam

BuschekBooks
Ottawa

Copyright © 2011 Doyali Farah Islam
All rights reserved.

Library and Archives Canada Cataloguing in Publication

Islam, Doyali Farah, 1984-
　　Yūsuf and the lotus flower / Doyali Farah Islam.

Poems.
ISBN 978-1-894543-66-8

　　I. Title.

PS8617.S53Y88 2011　　C811'.6　　C2011-902138-2

Cover design by Doyali Farah Islam, assembled by Patrick Soo.
Cover images
(top-left): part of "Yūsuf Entertains at Court Before His Marriage" from Jami's *Haft Awrang* (*Seven Thrones*). Freer Gallery of Art, Smithsonian Institution, Washington, D.C.
(top-right and bottom): "Lotus Flower" and "Water" by Laboni Islam

Printed in Winnipeg, Manitoba, Canada by Hignell Book Printing.

BuschekBooks
P.O. Box 74053, 5 Beechwood Avenue
Ottawa, Ontario, Canada K1M 2H9
www.buschekbooks.com

BuschekBooks acknowledges the support of the Canada Council for the Arts for its publishing program.

to the Divine, wherever the Divine dwells

Offerings

One | Commitment 7

thrust 9
I stand in earthiness recollecting 12
go as 13
I've felt progress 15
aaaamiiiin 16

Two | Character 17

captive 19
carrying 21

Three | Dignity 23

courage 25
Zamzam 27

Four | Divinity 29

someone 31
sangfroid (part i) 33
sangfroid (part ii) 34

Five | Grace 37

I have been 39
Muhammad 41
love provides 42
my brain unheel'd 43
pregnant 44
Yosef 46
Bilāl 48
young Yūsuf 50
conceive of this 52

Six | The Power to Sacrifice   53

? questions   55
what the lotus-eaters did not know   57
borrowed breath   59

Seven | Happiness   61

I am   63
…like   66
every atom   67

Notes   68

Glossary   73
Reflections   75
Credits   78
Gratitude: *Thank you to…*   80

One | Commitment

thrust

thrust,
a tiny key
into rusted heart-lock.

dig and twist.

saltwater rivers soften
russet cheeks. dis-
ease; tearing;
a shift in place.

I have fallen through something,
gouged a hole in a stable dam,
punctured murals of pastel skies and
watercolour'd sea.

I peer through, without my eyes.
now where am I?

        *

first light.
throaty drumming.
women croon ancient love and valour.

my body of disparate silt, sand, and
dust dreams water,
awakes to the clay of myself,
clutches for the first time a rope
(such a one was always here waiting)
finds I have a camel tied.

muscled thigh, arcing eye-
lash. my hump-ed burden unknots
my knowing.

water within reminds
my heart of what it seeks,
seeping healing, the greenness
of unsecret meeting,
slow roots sucking
through dirt, bountiful expansion.

I thirst, thirst,
for saturation.

the universal, human score:
I will return once more.

    *

once more, you too may return
with clarity to perfume the very core
of the seed within your soul,
the essence of which, pushed up slowly to surface
with one thousand indigo postures,
makes your face an open blossom—awesome,
unfolded lotus gleaming the sombre night,
come through the mud, come through the shit,
ever intoxicating and haunting in beauty.

saaaaaaaaaaaaaaaaaaaaaaaat naaam.
in duty, truth cannot be held back; truth
flowers open.

this wanting-more is my first admission;
the secret searing my breast.

    *

tiger-backed Kali sways up to the scene,
blushes as rusted iron breathes fertile ground.

in desert, something blooms,
becomes verdant.

stories here weave fresh roots.

routed along a carpet of stars,
Yūsuf is trundled south-west to Egypt.
Muhammad scrapes out of Mecca and steals to Medina.

these endings begin descanted
drops decanted from dawn, unstoppable.

my friend, such wine
has tipped many times.

line with me a path in song.

endings begin
descanted.

I stand in earthiness recollecting

I stand in earthiness recollecting
autumn in a Canadian wood:
burning, burning—alive in the burning;
churning, my heart-particles saw
destruction and creation unfold;
garnet, fire opal, amber, gold,
steel to copper to silver to gold.

so too did I tread steps into the neck of pines,
instantly wine-heady with remembrance—
the clean-smelling permeation of sap
that lengthened my look.

swathing seed to resilient lotus,
wildflower to blossom honey,
greenness of leaf dappled, and breathy,
sticky sap of wood pine—refreshing all,
and all telephone lines, signs striking calls
to loftiness; catalysts turning me toward devotion.

here, where I stand in renewal: invincible, bright
crispness of being, a natural clinging—yes,
everything gets stuck, becomes some of the
blessing; lightness that permeates, envelops, infuses,
the way menthol and eucalyptus kindle breath.

imagine the fragrant beauty
of the one who is
perfectly able to give all this.

go as

go as a pilgrim through life;
be unencumbered.

cloth of cotton white or wool—
one, two, pieces, no more
don't increase your burden.

diamond, ruby, jasper, jade—all
the trinkets of social affairs,
the glasses of social wares—
glitter ceasing in the light
of the dawn-time air.
leave that wine for another.

go as a pilgrim through life;
be unencumbered.

burdening traps,
booby traps, body wraps—burgeoning
insecurity when you pinch the fat,
rouge your lips and cheeks
like this, like that.

leave that thinness, that emptiness, that put-on rosiness,
for a thinness so thin it cannot be distinguished
from the whole, for a lover's blush
so deep the rose bows low.

lasting pilgrimage is not a mile outward, not
to Mecca,
to Medina,
to Amritsar—
not from physical-here to physical-there.

countless bare-footed steps
leave imprints rarer and subtler than that
upon the self.

tears for empty mounds
are no one's self-deliverance.

many lifetimes weeping,
with bone and sinew,
with grit and breath,
I have edged my self too close to freedom
to fall, back
into the prison chambers, back
into the previous layers, back
through 8.4 million cycles of *samsara*—
too far, lotus-bloom too near
to go back to bowing to any shit.

oh, my divine,
there can be no turning back;
this is it.

I will pluck the black clot out, this time
suck all of the black blood out.

go with me through veils,
beyond minarets, piercing spires,
domed rooftops, sun-struck ceilings—

set out, and quickly!

join me; venture where I am headed,
where Yūsuf and Ya'qūb embrace
in the flame of eternal love: old friends.

I've felt progress

I've felt progress swift as the sparrow
streaking lapis sky with Lazarusian wings.

given, she gives
pyrite stars their flame,
her song, a breath
of certainty.

other times, progress
is pain; I know. a broken—
mule staggering up the slope.
doubt, anger, fear, despair—I *know*.
don't think any soul submits without going
through this labour. payment is here already, not later.

…I sip freshness, when I pull water,
before bucket nears lips.

Yūsuf here lives
in attractiveness.

…I sit in the kitchen, start to shake
a glass bottle full of milk.

longing lightens.

before butter interrupts—*here I am!*—
something gives sweetness,
sustenance of all-I-need.

this, the greater miracle.

without separation, wholeness.

aaaamiiiin

aaaamiiiin;
amen;
hum;
aaaauuuummmm—
it's not loudness
that takes us home.

spit to seal a promise;
a black'd, perfume'd palm;
a blood pact—
all echo:

no friendship exists without trust.
no friendship exists without trust.
no friendship exists without
trust no friend without
friend,
something was whispered, and I bowed to it.

silent sanctity of commitment to every dawn:
a friend cannot help
but draw near, pour wine.

in the purification of your being,
the point will come
when you will no longer be held back
by whatever almost made you stay behind
and miss the blessing.

Two | Character

captive

captive in her love of Joseph,
Zulaykha awakes early:

what will make me irresistible?
air of lotus,
alluring felinity,
kohl-extended eye?

she draws from without;
dawn manifests the hidden.

the day billows by, keeping secret in its cheek
Zulaykha's ripening intent, praying that she shakes
moth balls from her skirt of dignity
and blows into safety, the way an innocent
schoolgirl scurries to draw up her knees
beneath the tented safety of an apple-red tarp
in a game of parachute.

        *

sun sinks disparaged out of crisp sky as
Joseph passes by, shine projecting.

as far away as Canaan
even his bloodied old rag of a shirt is wanting him!

the darkness of a high chamber-corner swoons, glows
to meet him. she pounces.

cat-claw at the mouse's back, she
tears his shirt in her wanting—
then lies to protect herself.

oh, how he wishes he could throw down a mantle
of honour over her.

some gems cannot be given.

when you too awake
and search for what will make you beautiful,
throw on the mantle of truth; cover yourself.

not keeping your word adds to the weight you owe,
swallows the light from your face.

even before his initiation, Muhammad was *al-amīn*,
his whole being radiant.

if you cannot afford the imprisoning burden,
the sinking shadow
—to be wretched-looking—
don't indulge the chain.

my friend, we both took the same covenant
once; sang the same praise-song.
we cannot endure the weight.

carrying

carrying the song of the divine
bushel'd between my arms
up to my throat,
like cyclamen gathered from rock under star,
spilling truth-song like a jar overflown,
my mouth over many sunset-angles
took on the taste of honey.

…is this what was meant when it was said
god gave nectar to the bees?

I am becoming
bee, and wildflower blossom;
nectar, and honey;
and you are drawn to my retiring mouth
just for that.

Ishmael, I become
soundless,
and everyone wants to tell me their secrets!

if I stay silent, I may hear
the divine speak to me
in even more tongues.

Ishmael, David is humming.

once a poor pied piper of lambs;
then a slayer of those inner things called goliaths;
now a king.

wrought king of iron,
he is buzzing psalms humbly
up and down the speaking hillside
and in the desert, with his throat-pipe,
followed by a wing-ed troupe
chorusing with the wind of glory,
huuuuuuuuuua!

Three | Dignity

courage
                courage [kər-ij]: from the Latin *cor*, meaning *heart*

when your heart and your hand
pass each other like strangers,
the cacophony between
clangs—*sadness*.

turn *that* way,
toward the echoes; oh,
turn that way.

weight of mud on flesh and blood:
I was a pig hampered by sludge, never lifting
my head or eyes; gleaning trough-feed
and scraps; for years, fattening myself up
for another cowardly death.

bacon, ham, loin, rib—
despairing primal cuts without ever sparing
my heart, that salve for our keen stings
of separation.

then you fed me curious
golden grain—faint
inner strains of music, tender chords
of heartstrings, lashing me to passage,
remembrance.

I tumbled with question
(until I returned polished with answer).

do we totter on some cosmic shelf
tied up together like nesting dolls—
outside, not silver bell but cockroach shell;
inside, soiled, bristled pig;
deep within, a being human,
deeper than that, a breathing soul?

there is a *you* who is,
a *you* who has always been
(worth more than scraps,
stronger than circumstance,
a beautiful creature of light.)

but no jewel shines with mud caked on;
no spirit-lamp guides with mud caked on.

take up your whetstone and draw the silver
(bow with courage).

the music that follows is surrender.

Zamzam

Zamzam was found
under a heap of dung,
where the blood of rites
fertilized stone.

…Zamzam …was found…
under a heap of dung.

it was ʿAbd al-Muṭṭalib
who decided which to cherish.

it wasn't just springwater,
but his decision
that was the freshness.

…this ground we unmuck
called listening heart
carves deep the shallowest
cup.

somewhere breathes its breath
from between your two breasts.

(no need to divine
perfect locations;
approximations are enough.)

…out in the plain open, I was searching for a particular thing,
and a thousand hidden
wellsprings of treasure
passed me by.

Hajar runs between two hills, desperate to find what quenches thirst.

then she gives up going back and forth in the desert of fear,
and Ishmael's heel strikes water.

Four | Divinity

someone

someone breathes within me.
I press the primal air.

am I drawn out of myself, and up, up?
burning, burning—hotly re-fired,
afloat and gusting with *Prān*—
do you clear my passage beyond,
beyond Shiraz, Konya, Andalusia,
beyond inky lines of limitations,
wrinkled lines of age and time,
back and back supremely
to your face itself?
...*su-param, su-param*...
where is my descent?

or am I pulled inward,
inwards in deep concentration,
to be fleshed out in secret, hidden
in an infant
...*al-bāṭin, al-bāṭin*...
in divine communion?

am I a sliver of silver moon and
wolf beneath, still prowling,
howling for full alchemy?

am I a moon-disc
retracing my steps and turns over fourteen nights,
becoming emptiness, fullness—
and with forefinger and thumb of a glov-ed hand,
slipping back behind the veil?

am I so full and bright, a gold moon-coin
at Shakti's shimmying hip,
swaying to and fro?
...*Aaadi Shakti, Aaadi Shakti, Aaadi Shakti, Namo Namo*...

do I have the slender grace of a gazelle's front leg
...*ghazalah, ghazalah!*...
and am I so sought, so beloved,
ancient woman, divine Shakti,
with climbing swirls of night'd hair?

in my perigeal swell or fade
I press the primal air...

let me brush back the slanting grass
from the forehead of the earth;
in nurture find a slant of glass,
a diamond face of your diamond face.

sangfroid (part i)

sangfroid while others swelter,
like Yūsuf, imprisoned,
you have made me no captive—
my grief-struggle bound to my destiny.

in each cramped cell,
a cupbearer for company.
converse with that one in secret.

my attraction swells,
like Yūsuf's vesture swirling out sober silks
blue-black and flapping a crescendo of attention
as from Zulaykha he tears toward an unseen
belov-ed. within

my wordless whining,
my thirst for calm union presses,
splits atoms, and I come uncoiled
as from stolidity infinity moves me.

I am a lotus wheel once stuck in mud,
petals centripetal, going back
into the primal origin of all things.

in my want, my wont—
chained again to you,
each golden link, my freedom.

sangfroid (part ii)

sangfroid while others swelter,
like Yūsuf, imprisoned,
you have made me no captive—
my grief-struggle bound to my destiny.

here with me, a cupbearer.
my old shirt torn, I slip on his.

but in confines I have no means
to present you wine
except by pressing myself.

and what vessel do I have
to offer this,
except myself?

thus I bring you a cup of your own drink,
straight to the lips that first made it
be!

so who offers to whom?

      *

even while I loved my husk
I was corn silk,
a green ear sold for paltry coins
to brighten here in prison.

advisor to the azīz;
a tuned and noble listener;
a sweetened ear—my personal harvest,
the divine heard breathing my lungs.

Zulaykha, I see your look,
when you pass my lightness by.

intrigued, mesmerized,
veil-shaved-thin;
no desire left
to be married to a shadow
of the true captain.

something more attractive than
rugged cheek, shoulder-breadth, even gold-
fleck'd clarity of eye,
calls you in:

jolted inside a worldly caravan,
wheels of wisdom turning,
you too are carted in a direction
that may make you dream ripening
and wake to merger.

life then: my throat closes,
cannot say its depth;
its sweetness—*wahe guru*.

Five | Grace

I have been

I have been who you are.
inside your sadness, thousands of times.

peering into your eyes, I
see myself.
you are who I am, too.

we are one hidden jewel
that pulls many faces
before facing our inner luminance.

savage, animal, shameful, low.
I have been what you are.

first we are seed,
cluster'd stars clutching
one light—fearless
in departure.

we sprout, lively and still
glassy-eyed with feverish remembrance,
but needy.

then we cool to shadow and mud
—shallow, forgetful, alone—
do things of which I need not speak…
(we who begin chains have done them, all).

if, by grace, we spot the light,
we call for breath
and expand into that
universe above.

petals bare light,
thin life's meaning to visible,
as the one exposed becomes the exposer.
(beauty manifests.)

Adam bit of the tree-fruit
and tasted compassion:
I understand temptation.

(one hundred and twenty-four thousand stories like this—
but most dissolved in silence.)

when you look into the eyes
of the drunkard you once were, remember
when you did not cup superior drunkenness.

love, agapé, will laugh your heart agape
instead of circling the realm.

Muhammad

Muhammad grew up arid, an orphan,
until milk overflowing found him—
the way nectar seeks the lotus centre
to be held by that breast
and given again
in love.

so this one, fragrant, sent of mercy,
poured his mantle over others.

don't ask me to explain it—
his bright cloak greening
the four directions,
like Gabriel the archangel
'compassing the horizon
so that you had to navigate
by the gut
or the starry north
of his eye.

stop your calculations, stop
mapping things out
with scrapings of reason.

navigate by that one—
        that one who—
        that one who offers—
re-orientation.

coming to compassion,
no human is left unwanted
(and every man is wanting
hu).

with heart medicine,
every lung is wanting
One—
and *no one* is left unwanted.

love provides

love provides
wellspring moisture
to thirsting, cracked clay:

winter, an un-lacquered shell;
we, the summertime seed inside
bursting forth joy,
firing the world kiln.

compassion:

a sheet of smudged glass,
wiped clear and cut
into a lens;

a mid-winter fleece;

amid lurid light, a sun-ray humble
warming the flesh of earth;

Abraham's granite water
bowl overflowing its rim
            without hot logic,
spontaneously,
in a desert waste.

abraham (human messenger)
  brahman (all-encompassing divine)
    raḥma (mercy)

        mercy, a divine message enacted,
            until it is the matrix of our marrow.

when flesh covers bone
are you *hu-*
man?

my brain unheel'd

my brain unheel'd is a
tense foot,
buzzing and bunching
the cloth of my knowing.

…when does dogged thought not
press upon initial trust?

help is hidden in this wearing.

a little more test,
a few more stitches
for my seams.

the finest dress of undress
is nakedly becoming.

…tearing forth heart-first,
I now pedal wakefulness.

the stuff that haunts those still in dreams
has no hold over me.

my skin,
a ripe date's, bursts the hem
of fear.

peeled of sticky doubt,
I can behave
like a lover:

divorced from the what-if mind,
impassioned,
for union, risking any venture.

pregnant

pregnant with love, pregnant
I pledged a covenant,
with a *yea!*—
bore promise of delivery.

Majnūn committed
to traces of Laylah;
madly I fell for shadow.

my pledge bound us—
but also made us separate,

the way *I do* can only happen
between two bodies.

…maybe I should have said (nothing),
but you asked me the question.

now I light myself on fire,
wrestle with heart-thorns.

I wish to be a belov-ed (bride);
what secateurs (to groom with)?

        *

I've seen the golden plate of earth,
how it spreads itself un-notch'd—
timeless though trunks of palm bear down
thinly with sun-dial shadows.

in this un-clock'd place,
Mary glows a secret (while)…
the mother of an unborn Muhammad
sees clear to Bostra.

when love conceives
to come full-term,
nothing obstructs.

our hearts, oases
we would otherwise dare not seek.

in a darkened wood, I do not keep
losing my direction;
I feel your presence here somewhere.

even shadow depends on light for existence.

Yosef

Yosef is down,
down,
down the well,
and we doubt that he remains
in beauty.

wildly Moses wanders for forty years,
and we wonder if we imagined
his golden arrival, his parting
of the sea.

swallowed whole,
forty days Jonah acquaints himself
with the cavern of a whale,
finding secret drink in that sealed-off tavern.

this is the testing time.

leave doubt behind
for what comes and goes
with purification.

*

a lover cries.

the more she yearns for wholeness,
the more holes she feels in the fabric of herself.

those rips at first seem small, of no import;
but with each passing night she mourns
the light that spills.

her yarn weaves another tale—listen:

such tears are slippery
darning needles, patching the invisible
frock of faith; and each
dropped saline stitch delights
the belov-ed's cheek.

    *

Abraham the Ḥanīf is busy
throwing himself on the fire.
or, w(h)etting the blade,
he understands what sacrifice brings
and walks straight toward—whose pain?

who-whoooo!
who-huuuuuuuuu!
hu-huuuuuuuuuuuuuu!

birds fly on wing unseen.

before that, they do not ask
if air will hold them.

    *

you too will break the bitter stretch
for embrace warm, unbroken.

inside you,
a pearl moon offers
to a string of dark horizon.

a small mouth kisses the ocean.

Bilāl

Bilāl   *balā'*   *balā*   !

black Bilāl
pinned beneath the boulder—

I am that one, one,
in the smoulder of a desert kiln,
scratching out stout pronouncements
from beneath the rock
—seemingly deserted—
left only in my tender skin.

will my chest withstand the crush?
therein I will find true release
beyond freedom bought
for the heavy jangle of gold.

Abu Bakr al-Ṣiddīq,
for what did my brother Yūsuf pass
into slavery?

something hidden, in question—
a precious pearl,
diamond, coral,
jasper, jade,
or clear water concealed
in a leather pouch.

pulled from my watery home,
I test the breadth of blazing sand.

there is wisdom in this,
my suffering.

as granite pestle bears down on petals
heavenly essence is exuded.

Yūsuf, too, knew it—
was pounded out, tested,
became gleaming gold leaf
bound again to water.

…one day I will chant for you
the newest of the ancient song;
make rooftops vibrate, lift up a *yea*,
and will call to you all
my bare feet steady,
my voice projected to the throng.
my body, still black and strong as proof
wrought from the soul's darkest night,
will throw back the black curtain
and show you dawn.

I will soon sing to you
in the chord of truth-love-courage
from a spool that provides unravelling light,
that you may cling
to the lyre-string of hope,
bear the crush
of clay by stone, and pressed
retrieve from depths
a sun-diamond to set on your crown.

young Yūsuf

young Yūsuf, o rosebud
in the waters of suffering;
cloaked in test,
never lost in shadow.

comely inside a corolla of insight—
rocks in a dry well polished themselves
just to reflect your beauty.

prismatic in prison,
enamoured locks squeezed tight
to bar your passage,
to keep your refractive face near.

here, in front of me, your many-coloured coat.

each hue reflects your inner
knowing, your patience and humility.

wanted by every hand,
you dreamt of sun, moon, stars—
never that you were beauty-giver.

but within your story, the promise
of an *insān* of *iḥsān*,
a beautiful humanity.

       *

in my loneliness, I cry out,
breath primal.
I cannot bear my ache.

prostrate: forceful rush of tears;
flung-open prison gate.

how humbleness cuts
sharply as a scimitar of bronze!

ego dashed;
life-blood once again flowing.

throwing on a white mantle, I bandage myself.
to myself, become invisible.

      *

here, balmy corolla(ries) with which to walk,
to make the way fragrant:

in suffering, sublime blessing.

in every rock—
in every rocky course—
there be the face of

god. you pierce me with my own thorns
and break me to make me whole.

conceive of this

conceive of this:

the less I am,
the more I gain.

when I enter paradox,
you are there.

longing constricts the vessel of self
until self becomes a seed.

in agony, I curled up,
so small, wet, and shaking with tears
that love at last   had space to enter.

resistance to help pierced,
I sang a forgotten song
with the cord of the womb:

allāhu akbar, allāhu akbar,
the the is greater, *the the* is greater.

at four I was pushed out as an infant,
bald, gurgling,
pale pink with mucousy dew,
cooing old love
to a blue sky.

I will crawl up the trellis now,
a salient rose,
and leave the air fragrant
just for your presence.

Six | The Power to Sacrifice

? questions

? questions
leap up from the flame of anger:

why existence,
why burden,
why toil?

something simmers, bubbles up, stirs shadow:

waḥy
       waḥy guru
            wahe guru
                —*wah!*

inspiration from within
      lighted inspiration
            here to guide me out of a dark cave, toward
                  ecstatic pronouncement—*wow!*

question laid to rest upon its side:
᭨ a ladle from soul to lip,
answer dished up:

we ring many circus acts
around love.

sip that broth;
take stock;
contemplate

what utter madness
we agreed to take on

when pure and unencumbered
we were in love with all that is divine.

meditate
on 7:172.

in love, we act lunatic:
sow our souls, all together;
resound without hesitation
balaaaaaaaaa.

I bear witness
to the foolish antics of love:

for love, Yūsuf threw himself down the well.
Abraham tore into fire.
for love, Jonah eyed the insides of the whale.
Jesus flung himself on the cross.

for love, Muhammad agreed
to be orphaned in childhood,
ridiculed in manhood;
and for no other reason but love, he served up,
poverty is my pride.

for love, Guru Tegh Bahadur lay down
for his beheading,
like Ishmael or Isaac prostrate upon the mount.

the rest of what you saw or heard—
Aurangzeb brocading a martyr's tale,
Quraysh throwing refuse on the supplicant Muhammad,
the haystack-whale hiding Jonah in its belly,
the mob wreathing the blaze set for twig-limb'd Abraham,
Yūsuf's ten step-brothers peering down the well:

all is invisible
love-labour, the play—
beings unaware that they, too,
were stirred by god.

what the lotus-eaters did not know

what the lotus-eaters did not know
was that the lotus itself was homeward.

so much so, the clinging
thought of home
clung flush to its brow.

imbibed, the flower's spinning head
unstopped for these men intoxication.

turning, they mixed going with ultimate place—
or was the conflation enlightened?

    *

listen, Yishay, o father of David:
how far stones and shepherds can travel.

against pastel skies, I was a pebble
into which darkness poured
from a curve of beach.

then some one swung up the scarf of night,
flung back the shade of sleep,
and cast my being
into dawn-filled sea.

    *

thinking waylaid me. I…

        skipped

for many lifetimes

        between

foetid air and sweet-flowing water,

      between

stagnation and transformation,

      between

seed of containment and open sowing.

unsure, flighty, darting—
a skittish stone, a vacillating eye;
I barely drew breath,
was blood congealed.

but show me a heart who can resist beauty.
(having fashioned me,
you will never stop seeking my beauty.)

what ear evades the all-compelling
strands of music that shatter stone
and draw soul to, reflective, lilting?

      *

I bel*onnnngggg* with you,
lend back my humanness,
and return my wending blood,
as the aged fruit of lotus
gives back its wholeness.

diving,
I split the ocean surface.

pebble becomes pearl through service.

borrowed breath

I am borrowed breath.
if you too are borrowed,
we meet in the home of our breather.

Seven | Happiness

I am

I am Ishmael's progeny, or Isaac's—
no matter.

the rock bares no name, but the face
is impressed
with the mole on the cheek
of the one who was awake
to sacrifice.

…into the cradle that cups my destiny
(that which you whispered all along
when I was not looking)
my tears that fall are beyond despair,
beyond ephemeral euphoria,
that short-lived joy, euphemerality.

suspension comes
—
jumping into this fire.

at your will, I drift in your infinite breeze:
dandelion seed head waiting to sow seed;
crepe paper streamers of kites colouring fair skies;
I flutter and float, fly onward into light.

      *

all of my previous slips of tongue,
fastidious pronouncements,
worldly soliloquies,
loose laughing entrances,
and gutted gasping exits
index'd
like cue cards relegated to dusty drawer
for no hand's reach,
no hand's reach.

my mouth at noon
—once clever and bright—
opens, closes
in the vacuum of departed speech:

flute-hole;
myna;
soul-fish;
lotus…

flute-hole that no longer knows its note to sing,
held by melodic bars within;

persimmon-beak'd myna gone
mute, lost for whistle and song;

silent fish unable to divulge secrets
to a waiting Moses;

dusk-and-dawn blossoming and retraction
of the flower of the lotus.

*

there is still work to do:
my *rūḥ* rushing still to
a destiny of strewn stars
that seed my open palm;
but what my hands make
is a small token
of the totality of the divine.
even in this—your breath within mine.

in the *sūq* of work,
I dip twine into paraffin and
display that candle, my mind…
…my mind captivated
by some other source of light…
here and not here.

*

Ishmael's progeny, or Isaac's—
no matter.

who am I except this?
no longer known;
as only a belov-ed can whisper,
wholly yours.

you've torn the shirt of my
capriciousness to rags;
and I exist no more
to look for Another.

…like

…like perfume lingering.
…like your lover's leaning-in for your ear.

somehow
I'm here.

here in this place
where analogy fails me.

where my mouth is the o
of closeness,
emptying still.

myein, my-in…
my index finger
turning slow.

Vishnu thinking *universe*.

a gyroscope spindle,
pointing to
a deliberate disc.

! only you can stop me
from making metaphor.

…that way, this.

every atom

every atom grinning with being,
I am a Jack sprung from my box,
free of all locks.

my grief rented as one thousand tears—
seed of lotus,
blossomed sustenance,
the-key-back-into,
merger.

blind-sighted Ya'qūb, o father of Yūsuf,
seed carrier, sewer, tender
who has yielded through the raking,
do you understand me?

in my tears, the salt of longing
dissolved into the vast ocean of love.

I was made as a clinging clot, singing salt,
searching for what to cling to.

then I found what divine self-
containment is,
how snow melts into its own spring.

now in my dancing step,
easy sway and bounce,
like supple branch of birch.

Notes

Yūsuf (Joseph): For a complete version of the Qur'ānic story of Yūsuf, turn to Abdullah Yusuf Ali's commentary on Sūrah Yūsuf (Sūrah 12) in his translation and exegesis, *The Meaning of the Holy Qur'ān: New Edition with Revised Translation, Commentary and Newly Compiled Comprehensive Index*. All Qur'ānic citations in these Notes use the tenth edition of Ali's work, courtesy of amana publications.

thrust

I will return once more: Lyric from "Land of the Silver Birch."

Kali…iron: 1) Kali is the Hindu goddess that "represents both aspects of maternal care, giving life in birth and receiving the dying" (Schmidt 236). She is often depicted riding a tiger or lion. 2) Also refers to the Kali Yuga or Iron Age in which consciousness is extremely dim and "religion and morality are in steep decline" (Schmidt 212).

go as

8.4 million cycles: The concept of reincarnation belongs solely to the Indic faiths. However, in both Indic and Abrahamic faiths, the experience of being human is precious.

black clot: Recalls a story about Muhammad's childhood, in which angels split open his chest and remove a black clot from his heart (Lings 26).

aaaamiiiin

a black'd, perfume'd palm: Refers to Muhammad's part in the pact of The Scented Ones (Lings 32).

carrying

Ishmael: The Biblical name of Abraham's eldest son means "God shall hear" (Lings 1). The Arabic name *Ismā'īl* with its tri-root—s m '—also indicates listening.

David: From the Qur'ānic perspective, David was a prophet and messenger of God. Ali notes that David is attributed with being the first person to make iron "coats of mail" (34:10-11, note 3800).

Zamzam

Zamzam...stone: While the "heap" element is hyperbolic, 'Abd al-Muṭṭalib did locate the spring of Zamzam near the Ka'bah at the site upon which he found dung, an ant's nest, as well as blood from ritual sacrifice performed by the Quraysh (Lings 10-11).

wellsprings of treasure: Refers to the history behind the Well of Zamzam —a well that was in use from the time of Ishmael and Hajar's story (explained below), until it was filled with the treasures of pilgrimage offerings by the Jurhumites who controlled Mecca (Lings 4). The Jurhumites covered the well with sand, and the water source was largely forgotten (Lings 5). Many years later, Muhammad's grandfather, 'Abd al-Muṭṭalib, sleeping near the Ka'bah, heard the Divine command, "Dig Zamzam!" (Lings 10). The well was recovered, and it still serves Muslim pilgrims on Hajj.

Hajar...strikes water: Hajar (Biblical: Hagar), the second wife of Abraham, after Sarah, was alone in the desert with her baby, Ishmael. Desperate to find water, she ran between two hillocks—now called Ṣafā and Marwah—so that she could view the desert from better vantage points. After seven tries with no sight of a caravan, she gave up and sat down. A well sprang up where Ishmael's heel touched the ground (Lings 2-3).

sangfroid (part i)

uncoiled: "[T]he kundalini, the soul nerve,...is coiled in three and a half circles" and can be "awakened" (Bhajan 21-22).

golden link: In Kundalini Yoga, the "golden chain" links student to teacher for protection and spiritual strength (Bhajan 54). In Sufism, too, a *silsila*—literally, a "chain"—of spiritual lineage connects disciple to master, all the way back to the Prophet Muhammad (Schimmel 169, 234).

sangfroid (part i and part ii)

cupbearer: Double meaning: 1) In the Qur'ānic narrative of Joseph, the imprisoned Yūsuf encountered a fellow inmate who used to be the cupbearer to the Azīz (Pharaoh). 2) In Sufi metaphors, one meaning of the cupbearer is Allah, "the [O]ne whose attention one seeks to gain" (Baldock 77).

Muhammad

heart medicine: In Kundalini yoga, the Fourth Chakra is the Heart Chakra, and it is the seat of compassion. In combination with the verse about "the four directions," the medicine wheel of First Nations peoples may be relevant. This poem is indeed about care, provision, and healing at many levels—physical, emotional, and spiritual.

Yosef

birds fly on wing unseen: "Do they not observe the birds above them, spreading their wings and folding them in? None can uphold them except (Allah) Most Gracious" (Qur'ān 67:19).

Bilāl

Bilāl: The Islamic story of Bilāl: The black slave and Muslim convert Bilāl was being tortured by his polytheistic master. Despite his torture, Bilāl repeated, "The One, The One," in firm recognition of his faith in Divine oneness (Lings 79). This Divine oneness is the Islamic concept of *tawḥīd* (Schimmel 17). 'Abu Bakr, a close companion of Muhammad, was passing by while Bilāl was being tortured. He freed Bilāl (Lings 79).

my brother: This term refers to the Islamic custom of addressing fellow Muslim men as *brothers* and fellow Muslim women as *sisters*. Bilāl was not related to Yūsuf through blood kinship, but in faith they were both in submission to one God.

yea: This yea refers to the Day of Alast (the Day of the Primordial Covenant) described in 7:172 in the Qur'ān, in which God gathered all of the seeds of human creation before their birth and asked, *alastu bi-rabbi-kum* (Am I not Your Lord?). The response was a resounding, *balā* (Yea!). The implication is that each soul, of its own free will, has made a conscious pact with the Divine. Each human is thus fully accountable for his or her actions in this temporary worldly plane. Furthermore, this covenant (*mīthāq*) always includes experiencing and withstanding trials and tribulations. See also Ali's notes 1146 – 1147.

lyre-string of hope: Allusion to George Frederic Watts's painting, "Hope" (1885). The more hidden reference is to the Qur'ānic verses which say, "…hold fast, all together, by the Rope which Allah (stretches out for you)" (3:103).

bear…diamond: The analogy of the diamond implies that consciousness is something to attain through a process of compaction under the pressure of human struggles, trials, and burdens (Singh).

clay: Islamic story of the Divine act of creation, in which God took "sounding clay," "moulded [this mud] into shape," and "breathed [the Divine] spirit into" the first human being—Adam (Qur'ān 15:28-29).

crown: Inner nobility is hard-earned. Also, the Crown Chakra (Seventh Chakra) connects us to the Divine. This chakra "has the key characteristic of surrender—the humility that fills you as you bow before the Infinite. That is one of the reasons that so many different traditions use the act of bowing" or prostration (Bhajan 194).

young Yūsuf

face: "withersoever ye turn, there is Allah's countenance" (Qur'ān 2:115). Ali notes that the Arabic word *wajh* "means (1) literally face, but it may imply (2) countenance or favour, [and] (3) honour, glory" (note 114).

conceive of this:

the the: The Arabic word *allāh* comes from the word *al-ilāh*, meaning *the god*. However, scholarship suggests that *ilāh* originates in an older word meaning *the*. Thus *allāh*, the Islamic and all-encompassing name for the Divine, could also convey the notion of that which is the Most Definite.

? questions

waḥy guru: Word play: a combination of Islamic and yogic words (see Glossary).

7:172: Again, Qur'anic reference (explained above in the note, "*yea*," for the poem "Bilāl").

Jesus flung himself on the cross: Crucifixion is predominantly a Christian belief.

poverty is my pride: An Islamic ḥadīth.

the mob...Abraham: The allusion is to a part of the Islamic story of Abraham (Arabic: Ibrāhīm). The idol worshippers, enraged because the young Abraham had smashed their temple idols, threw him into a great fire (Sarwar 152–153). The fire, to their disbelief and dismay, became cool and did not harm him (Sarwar 153).

I am

at noon: Alludes to the moment when the sun is at its zenith, but also to the homophonic Arabic letter *nūn*, which has associations with the Sufi state of annihilation (Schimmel 416).

...like

Vishnu: The Hindu deity of preservation and protection, associated with the quality of being all-pervading. Vishnu is often depicted with four arms—one of which carries a discus and another of which carries a lotus.

every atom

blind-sighted: Ya'qūb (Biblical: Jacob) was so distraught over the loss of his son, Yūsuf, that his weeping blinded him physiologically (Qur'ān 12:84). Yet Ya'qūb had the spiritual insight to understand that wisdom lay within his experience of separation (Qur'ān 12:86).

Glossary

adi shakti, adi shakti, adi shakti, namo namo (Gurmukhi) (Kundalini Yoga): I bow to the Primal Power

al-amīn (Arabic) (Islam): the Reliable, the Trustworthy, the Honest: a name bestowed upon Muhammad by his Meccan trade partners (Lings 34)

al-bāṭin (Arabic) (Islam): The Hidden (one of the 99 names of Allah)

āmīn (Arabic) (Islam): signifies trust in Allah

balā (Arabic) (Islam): yea; oh yes; but of course (used after a negation). See Qur'an 7:172.

balā' (Arabic) (Islam): suffering, trial, tribulation, affliction, distress

ghazalah (Arabic): female gazelle

hu (Arabic) (Sufism): the heartfelt Divine; a vibration of Divine remembrance.

iḥsān (Arabic) (Islam): "The Koran speaks of *islām* and *īmān*: *islām* is the complete and exclusive surrender of the faithful to God's will and [the individual's] perfect acceptance of the injunctions as preached in the Koran, whereas *īmān*, 'faith,' constitutes the interior aspect of Islam… As to *iḥsān*, it was added—according to most traditions by the Prophet himself—with the meaning "that you worship God as if you see [God]" (Schimmel 29). Grammatically, all three words are fourth-form Arabic maṣdars, *iḥsān* being from the tri-root—*ḥ, s, n*—which implies beauty.

insān (Arabic): "humankind," "human being," "person," "someone": the term is "gender non-specific" and reflects the "intricate gender balance within the Qur'ān" (Sells 37).

man (Sanskrit): mind

myein (Greek): to close one's lips and eyes

oṅg (Gurmukhi) (Kundalini Yoga): a creative vibration

rūḥ (Arabic) (Islam): spirit; breath of life; human life

sat nām (Gurmukhi) (Kundalini Yoga): I am truth; Truth is my identity

su-param (*supra-:* Latin; *param:* Sanskrit): beyond parameters: relates to the word *supreme* (Singh)

sūq (Arabic): market

wahe guru (Gurmukhi) (Sikhism; Kundalini Yoga, respectively): Wonderful Dispeller of Darkness; a mantra of ecstasy and elevation

waḥy (Arabic) (Islam): inspiration from within

Reflections

A Thematic Introduction: Motifs

Yūsuf and the Lotus Flower intertwines two key motifs, from which the title of the book emerged. Yūsuf (the Arabic name for Joseph) is a figure common to all three Abrahamic traditions. He is especially beloved by Sufis. The lotus is common to Hindu, Jain, Buddhist, Sikh, and yogic philosophy. In distinct ways, both motifs symbolize beautiful tenacity throughout hardship.

Creative Intentions

This poetry collection is a bridge of verse, a weaving-together of seemingly disparate spiritual paths. I draw conceptually from Eastern and Western traditions to convey my spiritual sentiments, insights, movements, and alchemical transformations. I incorporate formal elements of Indic worldviews—such as concepts of *samsara*, cyclical time, *karma*, and reincarnation. I remember, in verse, Islamic narratives—including those about Yūsuf and Zulaykha (Joseph and Potiphar's wife), Abraham, Hagar, Jonah, David, Moses, and Muhammad. While my shifts between spiritual worldviews might seem contradictory or even blasphemous to some, juxtaposition can amplify one's understanding of and devotion to any particular tradition.

For practitioners of faith, invocations of respect, such as the blessing "Peace be upon him," are implicit. They are absent in the poems for aesthetic reasons. Furthermore, if there are any factual mistakes or spiritual misguidances in this collection, I did not intend them.

Notes on Creative Process and Structure

The verses in this book manifested over the course of two years, during which time I sustained a daily practice of Islamic prayer and Kundalini yogic meditation.

Yūsuf and the Lotus Flower is a seven-part work, and the sections take their titles from Yogi Bhajan's list of Seven Steps to Happiness. I use these seven stages of commitment, character, dignity, divinity, grace, the power to sacrifice, and happiness as approximate markers on my inner spiritual journey.

We can think of the first step as the one that is required to reach the stage of commitment. The seventh step then becomes the one that moves us into joy. Alternatively, perhaps happiness is, in itself, a step toward something else.

Interestingly, the pen-to-paper arrival of the poems corresponded unintentionally with the chronology of Bhajan's Seven Steps. Only in retrospect did I divide the book up into its formal sections. Some poems seem to cross between sections, and this is natural, given the fluidity of inner alchemy. In particular, I find that each section revisits the first step of commitment in its own way, since renewed conscious commitment is a prerequisite for further inner progress. One does not commit once but many times over. In a similar way, I sense that one can undergo many cycles of these seven steps—each time experiencing a deepening of one's faith and joy. I have felt these cycles unfold in my own life.

A Perspective on the Notion of Translation

Poets are indeed great observers—of outward and inward states, processes, and dynamics. As "thrust," the first poem in *Yūsuf and the Lotus Flower*, sets out, my "peer[ing]" in this book is a task that happens primarily "without my eyes." However, I invoke and evoke sensory experiences to locate my observations in space and time. This concretization process is a process of Translation, although we might not primarily consider translation in this way. Most commonly, we think of translation as the act that converts one set of linguistic symbols into another, rather than the act by which the inclinations, longings, and dances of the soul are converted into word-symbols.

Insights into Listening, Recitation, and Reading

These verses are meant to be listened to, voiced aloud, and/or read in quietude. The message from poet Etheridge Knight is stunning: "The words from my mouth are beating on the drum of your ear, so don't take this as casual." Vocal intonation can create intimacy between the reciter and the creative artist. Many spiritual traditions, including Islām, encourage orality. It is often through recitation that sacred and spiritual verses come to be imprinted on and preserved in the metaphysical heart —in turn, transforming and preserving the reciter in subtle yet profound ways.

Final Thoughts

In a post-9/11 world, I have realized self-reflexively that my book highlights the gentle faces—both historico-scriptural and figurative—of Islām, Īmān, and Iḥsān. However, I am a lover of all journeys and streams that lead back to the Divine ocean. There are many traditions that I could not include explicitly in this book or as much as I would have liked, as these traditions did not relate neatly to my two main motifs. I hope that persons of these, as well as other, traditions can make apt connections to their own values and systems of meaning. I also hope that, in some small way, I have contributed to a boundless vision of peace, love, friendship, and harmony.

There is endless delight in poetry.

Salām, Sat Nām, Khudā Ḥāfiẓ.

Doyali Farah Islam
Toronto, Canada

Credits

Front Cover Image (top-left):
"Yūsuf Entertains at Court Before His Marriage" from Jami's *Haft Awrang* (*Seven Thrones*). Freer Gallery of Art, Smithsonian Institution, Washington, D.C.: Purchase, F1946.12.132r. With permission.

Front Cover Images (top-right and bottom):
"Lotus Flower" and "Water" by Laboni Islam. With permission.

The Meaning of The Holy Qur'ān, English translation by Abdullah Yusuf Ali (Beltsville, Maryland, amana publications, 2010). With permission.

Baldock, John. *The Essence of Sufism*. Arcturus Publishing Limited: London, 2004. With permission.

Copyright 2003. Bhajan, Yogi. All teachings, yoga sets, techniques, kriyas and meditations courtesy of The Teachings of Yogi Bhajan. Reprinted with permission. Unauthorized duplication is a violation of applicable laws. ALL RIGHTS RESERVED. No part of these Teachings may be reproduced or transmitted in any form by any means, electronic or mechanical, including photocopying and recording, or by any information storage and retrieval system, except as may be expressly permitted in writing by the The Teachings of Yogi Bhajan. To request permission, please write to KRI at PO Box 1819, Santa Cruz, NM 87567 or see www.kriteachings.org. Quotations come from *The Aquarian Teacher*.

Knight, Etheridge. Quotation as remembered and related by Michael Meade. With permission.

Muhammad: His Life Based on the Earliest Sources by Martin Lings, Inner Traditions / Bear & Co. © 1983, 1991, 2006, originally published in the UK by George Allen & Unwin © 1983 With permission.

Sarwar, Ghulam. *Islām: Beliefs and Teachings*. The Muslim Educational Trust: London, 1996. With permission.

Schimmel, Annemarie. *Mystical Dimensions of Islam*. The University of North Carolina Press: Chapel Hill, 1975. With premission.

From SCHMIDT ET AL. *Patterns of Religion*, 1E. © 1999 Wadsworth, a part of Cengage Learning, Inc. Reproduced by permission. www.cengage.com/permissions

Sells, Michael. *Approaching the Qur'ān: The Early Revelations*. White Cloud Press: Ashland, 1999. With permission.

Singh, Shiv Charan. Insights into the analogy of the diamond and the etymology of the word *supreme*. With permission.

Gratitude: *Thank you to...*

John Buschek, for your willingness to take a chance on the unknown voice of a young Canadian writer.

Sylvia Legris. Your responses during our correspondence have given me new considerations with which to approach my craft. Your interest in my work has gifted me with more confidence in my literary voice.

Dr. Todd Lawson, for your support and encouragement.

Patrick Soo. I could not have executed my vision for the front cover without your skill or generosity with time.

my mother. You have given me an embodied example of ceaseless hard work, positivity, and immense sacrifice. Thank you, also, for providing me in childhood with the tools of creativity: paper, colours, time.

my father. You have impressed upon me the insight that we own nothing—that everything belongs to God. Your acumen, including your ability to take a long view of time, never ceases to amaze me.

Laboni Islam. True to your name, you are grace. Thank you, also, for your brilliant pencil crayon illustration of the lotus as well as for the careful brushstrokes of wave and shore that appear on the front cover.

Andrew Bernard Lamar. Your love enfolds me and safely keeps me.

*

Praise, thanks, and glory be to Allah, the Divine who has many names. I call upon You as the loving and protecting friend, the best of all planners, the one who humbles.